Birthdays Around the World

by Jay Dale

illustrated by Cherie Zamazing

We all have a birthday.

2

HAPPY BIRTHDAY

3

This is my family.

They are all here for my birthday.

We will have a party with hats and balloons.

We will have a cake, too!

cake

An American party

This is my family.

They are all here for my birthday.

We are going to eat sweet cakes.

We are going to the *temple*.

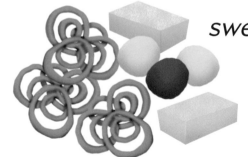

sweet cakes

6

An Indian party

This is my family.

They are all here for my birthday.

We are at the temple.

I am in my good clothes.

kimono

A Japanese party

This is my family.
They are all here for my birthday.
We are going to have
a very big party.
I will hit the *piñata* with a stick.
We will see candy come out!

piñata

A Mexican party

11

This is my family.

They are all here for my birthday.

We will eat a cake.

In the cake are *eggs* and *potato*.

We will *dance* and *sing*.

cake

A Ghanaian party

13

We all have a birthday.
You have a birthday, too!

Picture Glossary

dance

eggs

piñata

potato

temple